Virtual Reality in Retail

Revolutionizing Shopping Experience

Table of Contents

1. Introduction 1

2. Understanding Virtual Reality: A Simplified Approach 2

   2.1. A Brief History 2

   2.2. VR Today: More than Entertainment 3

   2.3. Understanding VR: The Basics 3

   2.4. VR and Augmented Reality: Spot the Difference ... 4

   2.5. How Does VR Work? 4

   2.6. The Future is Virtually Here 4

3. Tracing the Evolution of Retail: From Brick-and-Mortar to VR 6

   3.1. The Era of Brick-and-Mortar Stores 6

   3.2. The Age of E-commerce 6

   3.3. Demystifying Virtual Reality (VR) 7

   3.4. The Emergence of VR in Retail 8

   3.5. The Present and Future of Retail: VR Stores 8

4. Virtual Reality in Retail: A Potential Game Changer 10

   4.1. The Introduction To Virtual Reality in Retail 10

   4.2. The Mechanism - How Does It Work? 11

   4.3. VR's Increasing Presence in Retail 11

   4.4. Why is VR the Future of Retail? 12

   4.5. The Abyss - Challenges of VR in Retail 12

5. Bridging Gaps: VR's Role in Omnichannel Retailing 14

   5.1. The Genesis: Why VR in Omnichannel Retailing? ... 14

   5.2. The Intersection: How Does VR Contribute? 15

   5.3. VR at Work: Progressive Examples in the Industry ... 15

   5.4. The Road Ahead: VR's Future in Omnichannel Retail ... 16

6. Artificial Intelligence and VR: A Perfect Retail Blend 18

   6.1. AI: Enhancing Core Aspects of VR 18

      6.1.1. Personalized Recommendation 18

6.1.2. Improved Search Functionality 19

6.2. VR: Creating Experiential Retail 19

6.2.1. Virtual Store Tours 19

6.2.2. Product Trials 19

6.3. The AI-VR Symbiosis in Retail 20

6.3.1. Immersive Retail Environments 20

6.3.2. Real-time Customer Support 20

7. Changing Consumer Behaviours: The VR Effect 22

7.1. The New Paradigm: Shopping through VR 22

7.2. The VR Effect on Purchase Decisions 23

7.3. Cultivating Brand Image and Loyalty 23

7.4. Looking Ahead: The Future of Shopping Behaviour 24

8. Future Prospects: The Next Big Things in VR Shopping 26

8.1. Unshackled Shopping - Walking the Aisles Virtually 26

8.2. Tailored to Fit - Virtual Fitting Rooms 27

8.3. An Augmented Reality - Revolutionizing Product
Interactions 27

8.4. Personalized Shopping Assistants 28

8.5. A More Inclusive Shopping Experience 28

8.6. Streamlining the Supply Chain 28

8.7. Rethinking Advertisement and Marketing Strategies 28

8.8. Conclusion 29

9. Obstacles in VR Adoption and Their Potential Solutions 30

9.1. Technological Limitations 30

9.2. User Experience and Usability 31

9.3. Content Creation and Curation 31

9.4. Health and Safety Concerns 32

9.5. Societal Acceptance 32

10. Case Studies: Successful Applications of VR in Retail 33

10.1. IKEA: Design Your Dream Home 33

10.2. Lowe's: Holoroom How To ... 33

10.3. Audi: VR Showrooms ... 34

10.4. Alibaba: VR Shopping ... 34

11. Endless Aisles: The Virtual Shopping Experience of Tomorrow . 36

11.1. Immersive Worlds Crafted around the Consumer ... 36

11.2. Revolutionary Product Interaction ... 37

11.3. 'Smart' Personalized Recommendations ... 37

11.4. Enriching Social Interactions ... 38

11.5. Overcoming the Barriers ... 38

Chapter 1. Introduction

Dive into an immersive spectacle of possibilities with our Special Report: "Virtual Reality in Retail: Revolutionizing Shopping Experience". No need for tech-savviness, we make it approachable and fascinating for everyone! Unravel the transformative potential of Virtual Reality (VR) in reshaping one of mankind's oldest activities - shopping. Witness the retail spectrum being rewritten beyond normal comprehension while making it all the more engaging, convenient, and downright exciting. We promise this read will have you captivated, teeming with anticipation about the shopping evolution that's not in some distant future, but right around the corner. If you've ever dreamed about where technology can take us, strap in and let's explore the realm of Virtual Reality in Retail together, in this venture, we're sure every word is worth your dime!

Chapter 2. Understanding Virtual Reality: A Simplified Approach

Virtual reality; two simple words that hold an astonishing degree of promise and potential. However, the understanding of what virtual reality truly is, isn't as widespread, which is where we aim to bridge the gap. As we navigate this space, you will find your understanding and perspective unraveling to accommodate this novel idea - an idea that's set to change the world as we know it.

2.1. A Brief History

Virtually real? Real virtually? The concepts now packaged neatly in the term "Virtual Reality" have occupied human imagination for centuries. The earliest known immersive multi-sensory experience was Panorama Mesdag, designed by one Hendrik Willem Mesdag. A cylindrical painting, it immersed visitors in an illusion of reality. Fast forwarding to the latter part of the 20th century, in the late 1960s, Ivan Sutherland's "Sword of Damocles", the first head-mounted display (HMD), appeared, wielding an uncanny resemblance to modern VR devices.

Over the intervening years, Virtual reality became a darling of the entertainment sector, experiencing stints of soaring popularity and troughs of disillusionment. However, it was arguably the 21st century that truly marked the beginning of what we now know and understand as VR.

2.2. VR Today: More than Entertainment

The modern incarnation of VR is vastly more sophisticated than its early forebears. The hardware has evolved; it's lighter, more immersive, and significantly less expensive. Today, VR isn't just about gaming or immersive cinema experiences. It's being used in healthcare, real estate, architecture, and more pertinently, retail.

Virtual reality has the potential to transform the retail industry by creating immersive experiences that bridge the gap between the convenience of online shopping and the tactile satisfaction of physical stores. Customers can now try items, witness how they work or feel, and make better-informed decisions — all within the comfort of their homes.

2.3. Understanding VR: The Basics

To understand Virtual Reality (VR), we must first break down the term. Virtual signifies something close to reality, and Reality is our experienced existence. Therefore, Virtual Reality refers to experiences close to reality but created artificially by software. VR works by simulating our senses such as vision, hearing, touch, and even smell. This simulation tricks our mind into accepting the virtual environment as real.

The central hardware in VR is the Head Mounted Display (HMD). Accompanied by headphones for sound, some VR systems also come with handheld devices that allow you to interact with the virtual environment.

2.4. VR and Augmented Reality: Spot the Difference

Virtual Reality often gets spoken in the same breath as Augmented Reality (AR) due to their shared ability to alter our perception of the world. However, they aren't the same. AR overlays digital data on real-world elements, allowing interaction with both, while enhancing real-life experiences. AR is used in mobile games like Pokémon Go or apps like Snapchat. On the other hand, VR creates a complete immersion experience that virtually takes you out of the physical world and into a digital realm.

2.5. How Does VR Work?

VR tricks the human brain into believing it's somewhere it is not. This is achieved by two autofocus lenses placed between the screen and the eyes adjusted to frame the screen. When these adjustable lenses are positioned correctly, they create a stereoscopic 3D image by angling two 2D images to mimic how human eyes perceive the world around us.

2.6. The Future is Virtually Here

We've come a long way in understanding and developing Virtual Reality. Initial trials and errors have not only shaped our current understanding, they have also launched us into the future of possibilities. VR in the retail industry is no exception. Already shaping up to be a game-changer, this technology brings the promise of not only transforming shopping experiences but potentially rewriting the landscape of retail as well.

So, as we stand on the precipice of the new world, it's important to understand the foundations on which VR is built. The hardware, the software, the design principles – all these aspects tied together give us the phenomena known as Virtual Reality. Join us as we dive further into the mechanisms of VR and dig deeper into its potential to revolutionise the spectrum of the retail industry.

Chapter 3. Tracing the Evolution of Retail: From Brick-and-Mortar to VR

In the history of retail, it all started with the simple exchange of goods for other goods or services, a system formally recognized as bartering. This changeable form of trading catalyzed the advent of stores, laying the foundation for the brick-and-mortar shopping experience we're all familiar with.

3.1. The Era of Brick-and-Mortar Stores

Centuries ago, the earliest of marketplaces - agora in Greece, forum in Rome - were established, becoming central locations where vendors could sell their goods directly to consumers. Whatever the period or place, people desired a physical place to shop. It was here that one could touch, feel, and inspect items before committing. Such in-person exchanges continued to dominate buying behavior for hundreds of years.

Fast forward to the 18th and 19th centuries as the concept of retail became more sophisticated with the evolution of department stores. The first department store, Le Bon Marché, opened its doors in 1852 in Paris, revolutionizing retail by gathering an impressive variety of goods under one roof. This tradition became standard and remains central to the retail industry today.

3.2. The Age of E-commerce

In the late 20th century, retailers made a significant leap from the physical to the digital world. It all started when English inventor Michael Aldrich connected a television set to a transaction processing computer with a telephone line, and e-commerce was born.

When the internet became accessible to ordinary people, businesses were quick to identify its potential. In 1994, Jeff Bezos used this new platform to launch Amazon - initially a humble bookselling venture. Soon enough, though, companies across the globe were exploring ways to digitize their operations, marking the beginning of the e-commerce boom.

Thanks to companies like eBay and Amazon, products previously available only at brick-and-mortar stores became accessible from homes. Suddenly, the need to physically visit a store started becoming optional. Online shopping offered the added convenience of delivering products right to the customer's doorstep. The introduction of secure payment gateways bolstered trust, promoting further adoption of e-commerce.

However, e-commerce had its drawbacks - the lack of 'real' shopping experience being chief among them. Although online, customers couldn't touch or try products making decisions hinge more heavily on images and product descriptions. The rise of advanced technology took on the task of tackling these challenges head-on. One such promising technology has been Virtual Reality (VR), with the potential to bridge the gap between brick-and-mortar and e-commerce shopping experiences.

3.3. Demystifying Virtual Reality (VR)

Initially, VR was primarily linked to the gaming industry, providing gamers a more immersive and interactive experience. Soon though, other sectors recognized VR's potential, one of them being retail.

VR is a computer-generated 3D environment that can be interactively explored by the user. By putting on a VR headset, users are transported to a virtual world that offers an experience almost as real as the physical world. The critical aspect of VR is immersion - creating a deep sense of physical presence in a non-physical world.

3.4. The Emergence of VR in Retail

The integration of VR into retail began as a solution to e-commerce's major drawbacks. However, with enhancements in technology and accessibility, VR began offering much more.

Several early adopters of VR in retail aimed to recreate the physical store experience virtually. For instance, Alibaba introduced Buy+, a VR shopping experience. Users could wear VR glasses to navigate through a virtual shopping mall and select items on display, similar to a physical shopping experience.

VR also enabled retailers to offer customizable experiences. IKEA's VR experience allows users to design their kitchen by selecting and placing items while walking around the virtual kitchen just like they would in their own home.

VR brought much-needed novelty and excitement to shopping, something that was gradually fading in physical and online shopping experiences. Such experiences continue to evolve even today, persistently blurring the lines between the physical and virtual realms of retail.

3.5. The Present and Future of Retail: VR Stores

The tremendous potential of Virtual Reality in retail became clearer as the technology evolved and became more accessible. Its immersive nature opened previously unimaginable avenues, offering experiential product demos, virtual shopping assistants, and personalized shopping sessions.

Immersive product demonstrations, a potent application of VR, have gained significant popularity. For instance, car dealerships can offer virtual test drives that highlight features and mimic the driving experience.

As of now, VR stores still coexist with brick-and-mortar and online shops. However, it won't be surprising with further advancements and wider acceptance, VR could become the prominent platform for shopping in the near future.

Crucially, now is the optimal time for retailers to adopt this futuristic approach. Early adoption of VR technology could be pivotal in capturing a significant segment of the market and building a sturdy customer relationship.

VR could very well be the next big thing in retail, redefining the industry as we know it. As it evolves and expands, it promises to provide an engaging, personalized, and highly interactive shopping experience that's much more than just a transaction - it's a transformation. With VR, shopping comes full circle, offering the convenience of e-commerce and the palpable charm of physical stores, delivering something not just better, but revolutionary. The retail industry is poised for one of the grandest evolutions: from brick-and-mortar to VR. It's truly an exciting time to be a consumer!

Chapter 4. Virtual Reality in Retail: A Potential Game Changer

We live in rapidly evolving times. There isn't a field, sector or practice that hasn't been touched by the transformative nature of technology. This constant change continues to unsettle the status quo, reshaping our perceptions on how things traditionally worked. Let's script a new narrative, infusing innovative possibilities into an ancient activity of mankind - shopping. Brace yourself as we unravel the enthralling future of retail and shopping, powered by the magic of Virtual Reality (VR).

4.1. The Introduction To Virtual Reality in Retail

Virtual Reality (VR) isn't just about gaming or entertainment anymore. It has effectively breached the boundaries of its initial use-cases and started permeating various industries - one of which is retail. It resembles a digital carving of the real-world environment, manipulating your senses to teleport you to a universe that is governed entirely by simulation.

In retail, this means no more queues or crowded spaces; the hassles of physically going through hundreds of products or standing in billing lines are now problems of the past. Instead of enduring these inconveniences, imagine finding yourself in a 360-degree virtual space, meticulously constructed to provide an authentic shopping environment. This is no science fiction. It's a world that retail companies are striving to make a reality.

4.2. The Mechanism - How Does It Work?

VR uses a technology called 'Real-Time Rendering', which operates by swiftly converting 3d models into 2D images while incorporating textures, colors, lighting, and other factors. This technique tricks the human brain into perceiving these artificially rendered images as real-life environments. A computer (usually a high-resolution smartphone or VR equipment) generates these simulations, and using a VR headset, it provides an immersive user experience.

Upon wearing a VR headset, the user's movements - such as turning the head or walking in a direction - are tracked and translated into the virtual environment. This creates an illusion of navigating through a real space. It's a technology ensuring comfort while shopping and adding an entertainment factor to the usually mundane task.

4.3. VR's Increasing Presence in Retail

Brands worldwide are increasingly implementing VR to create memorable and delightful shopping experiences. A renowned example of VR retail done right is Alibaba's 'Buy+' mall, where shoppers can go through thousands of products across various shops simply by using a VR headset. IKEA, too, is pushing boundaries with their VR Kitchen Experience that allows their customers to remodel the kitchen digitally before making any actual purchases.

Even industries like automotive and real estate have dipped their toes into VR retail. Lexus's virtual showroom lets customers explore different models, customize features, all while the comforting veil of their homes surrounds them. Meanwhile, prospective home buyers can virtually tour properties using VR technologies, saving both time and commuting costs.

4.4. Why is VR the Future of Retail?

Beyond the novelty factor, several reasons warrant VR's indispensability in the future of retail. Firstly, the convenience it offers to customers. Who wouldn't want a simplified, immersive shopping experience from the comfort of their homes? Moreover, VR also mitigates the classic online shopping drawbacks like the inability to try products before buying them.

Secondly, it provides a means for retailers to differentiate themselves in an overcrowded market. As more and more consumers become tech-savvy, retailers who adopt innovative technology like VR are likely to outshine their competition.

Lastly, VR technology provides essential customer data for retailers. Behaviors, preferences, popular products - all this information can be collected and used to create a more personalized shopping experience, thus driving sales and customer satisfaction.

4.5. The Abyss - Challenges of VR in Retail

Like every technological innovation, VR in retail also presents its challenges. The high cost of VR equipment can deter many individuals and small businesses from adoption. Additionally, developing a successful VR interface requires significant time, resources and technical proficiency - another hurdle for many retailers. There's also the challenge of customer acceptance. Some customers may be reluctant to use this new technology, thinking of it as complicated or unnecessary.

However, as history has repeatedly shown, humans have a remarkable ability to adapt and embrace technological advancements. There were similar hesitations when online shopping was first introduced, and now, it has become a standard practice. VR, too, with improved accessibility and further advancements, is standing on the precipice of universal acceptance.

Despite the challenges, the potential rewards of VR in retail far outweigh the risks. It's a technology that offers benefits to both consumers and retailers alike, and with the right approach, it can revolutionize the shopping experience as we know it. Strap in, and let's stay tuned to witness a shopping evolution that's not in some distant future, but right around the corner!

Chapter 5. Bridging Gaps: VR's Role in Omnichannel Retailing

In the dynamic world of retail, the demand for an integrated multi-channel shopping experience continues to intensify. Digital and physical channels are no longer stand-alone platforms but, instead, parts of an overarching and harmonized experience. This is where the omnichannel approach to retail comes into play - blending both digital and physical forms of shopping into a seamless, unified experience for the customer. The role of Virtual Reality (VR) begins to unroll in this environment, transforming the shopping realm into an engrossing, interactive scenario, with a 'try before you buy' assurance.

5.1. The Genesis: Why VR in Omnichannel Retailing?

The omnichannel approach has steadily gained momentum due to several key elements. Chief among them, customer preferences have dramatically shifted towards a more integrated shopping experience that weaves together in-store, online and mobile touch points in harmony. As a result, businesses must adapt. This has opened the doors for disruptive technology like VR to take center stage.

In this context, VR is not merely another gimmick or an additional channel. It has the potential to bridge the gap between physical and digital, exponentially enhancing the omnichannel retail experience. Shoppers can immerse themselves in virtual environments, visualizing products, and make confident buying decisions based on rich, virtual experience.

Think about furniture shopping. Online images may not justify the product, and in-store visits might be time-consuming. VR solves this dilemma by bringing the product to life. You can virtually 'place' furniture in your home and determine if it suits your decor before buying. Comfort, convenience, and decision-making — VR delivers on all fronts, bridging the existing gaps in omnichannel retail.

5.2. The Intersection: How Does VR Contribute?

VR's contribution is two-pronged: enhancing the customer journey and enabling businesses to leverage shopper insights.

1. Customer Journey: VR helps create immersive customer journeys. It allows customers to interact with products in a virtual setup, providing them with a thorough understanding of the product. It significantly decreases the uncertainty around product features, dimensions, colors, and more, which are often the factors influencing shopping cart abandonment.

2. Shopper Insights: Businesses can collect and analyze customer behavior data from their VR interactions. This data can consist of the sections customers frequently visit, the products they interact with the most, the time they spend on each product, and much more. Such insights can help businesses fine-tune their offerings and strategies, ultimately maximizing customer satisfaction and sales.

5.3. VR at Work: Progressive Examples in the Industry

Several companies are actively incorporating VR into their omnichannel strategy. IKEA, for instance, has developed a VR app that lets users virtually remodel their kitchens. The app builds an immersive experience where users can walk around their virtual kitchen, open drawers, and even cook virtual food.

Lowe's, the home improvement company, has launched a VR tool called 'Holoroom How To'. This tool provides customers with a step-by-step guide to complete a home improvement project in a virtual environment before they attempt to do it in reality.

These are not just isolated examples. They signal an industry-wide recognition of VR's potential in enriching the omnichannel retail realm.

5.4. The Road Ahead: VR's Future in Omnichannel Retail

The initial applications of VR in retail suggest a promising future. Yet, the scaling of VR applications beyond novelty to normalized use is quintessential for it to transform omnichannel retailing fundamentally. Several trends and factors hint at this gradual transition.

1. Advancements in VR Technology: VR tech, as we know it today, will continue to evolve. The focus will shift towards refining VR headsets' performance and making them more consumer-friendly, comfortable, and affordable.

2. More Engaging Omnichannel Experiences: As businesses continue to aim for differentiated and delightful customer experiences, VR is likely to become a critical touchpoint in omnichannel retail. It's not hard to imagine a future where VR integrates seamlessly with other channels, giving businesses more control over customer experiences, and customers more interactive ways to shop.

3. Data-Driven Retail: The power of VR to furnish in-depth customer behavioral data will enable retailers to tailor offerings precisely,

thereby enhancing the shopping experience significantly.

4. Edge over Competition: As early adopters benefit from their VR ventures, others will join the folds to provide competitive customer experiences. This will continually push the envelope of how VR can influence omnichannel retailing.

The journey of VR in retail has just begun. The future indeed looks promising with VR poised to become the linchpin in the omnichannel retail experience. Bound to bridge gaps and confluence the digital and physical realms of shopping, VR stands firm as a catalyst for retail transformation. It will not only dictate how businesses operate but also redefine the essence of shopping, proving to be the ultimate harbinger of immersive consumerism. The revolution is not on the horizon; it is, undeniably, right here, right now.

Chapter 6. Artificial Intelligence and VR: A Perfect Retail Blend

It's a fascinating era where two of the most awe-striking technologies – Virtual Reality (VR) and Artificial Intelligence (AI) – are seamlessly converging to reimagine the world of retail. The power of their synergistic abilities is like nothing we've ever seen and is setting the groundwork for a shopping experience that's immersive, engaging, and fundamentally more human.

6.1. AI: Enhancing Core Aspects of VR

AI's integration into VR is creating a more enriching, personalized, and interactive shopping experience. Here is where the two transformative technologies intersect:

6.1.1. Personalized Recommendation

AI technology helps identify a customer's style, needs, and preferences through their shopping behavior and browsing patterns. By analyzing these data, AI can create a perfect, personalized shopping experience for each customer by curating a selection of goods and services the customer may prefer. When integrated into VR, users can enjoy a customized virtual shopping environment with recommended products that match their identified preferences ensuring a convenient and enjoyable shopping journey.

6.1.2. Improved Search Functionality

The right search feature is crucial in virtual shopping to make it easy and quick for customers to find what they're looking for. AI makes it exponentially easier for customers to find their desired item among hundreds of thousands of products. It recognizes shoppers' search behaviors and common search patterns to refine its algorithms. The result? A search functionality that understands and delivers exactly what the customer wants, providing far more accurate and relevant results.

6.2. VR: Creating Experiential Retail

The conventional retail industry has long been negotiating with the challenges of bridging the gap between physical stores and online platforms. With the advent of VR, a whole new style of experiential retail is emerging, focusing more on 'experience per square foot' instead of the traditional 'sales per square foot.'

6.2.1. Virtual Store Tours

Imagine having the privilege of leisurely walking around in your favorite store without leaving the comfort of your home, let alone your couch. This is what VR technology offers. Customers can have a 360-degree panoramic view of the store, walk around, and easily interact with products of interest.

6.2.2. Product Trials

Perhaps the most enthralling aspect of integrating VR into retail is the ability to virtually try products before buying them. Customers can inspect a product in detail and even perceive how a piece of apparel or accessory would look on them. It reduces uncertainties related with online shopping, thus improving customer's confidence in their purchases.

6.3. The AI-VR Symbiosis in Retail

It's clear that both VR and AI are essential pillars of the future retail experience. However, their complete potential can only be realized when they are used in conjunction where the combined power delivers a shopping experience beyond comparison.

6.3.1. Immersive Retail Environments

With AI/VR technology, retailers can develop highly interactive environments that can respond to customers' behaviors and preferences in real time. This means the ability to generate personalized product displays, adaptive store layouts, and responsive product details, all contributing towards creating a hyper-personalized multimodal shopping experience.

6.3.2. Real-time Customer Support

Integrating AI with VR enhances customer service by embedding virtual assistants into VR retail experiences. These AI bots can solve queries, provide product recommendations, and even guide customers towards their desired products, all in an immersive virtual environment. This makes the shopping experience more seamless, eliminating the need to exit the VR environment to seek assistance.

In summary, the convergence of AI and VR in retail is a game-changing blend that's transforming the paradigm of shopping. Connecting these two technologies takes us into a world where shopping isn't just about buying but an extraordinary and immersive experience in itself. The AI/VR amalgamation is creating a highly personalized, interactive, and engaging shopping environment, ensuring every customer's journey is unique, efficient, and nothing short of extraordinary.

Indeed, as we unlock greater potentials of AI and VR shepherded by relentless innovation, the retail industry stands on the precipice of a revolutionary transformation. A future where every physical act of shopping can be experienced virtually, with enhanced personalization and helpful assistance. The dawn of this transformative era in retail cannot be overstated - it is happening in the here and now, and we are privileged to witness the extraordinary ways in which AI and VR are reshaping the retail landscape forever.

Chapter 7. Changing Consumer Behaviours: The VR Effect

The dawn of the 21st century has been marked by rapid advances in technology, and one of these leaps forward has been the advent of Virtual Reality (VR). A technological marvel that has extended its influence in various walks of life, VR has opened doors to incredible possibilities, from gaming and entertainment to education and healthcare. The retail sector has not been left untouched. Redeeming the conventional shopping experience, VR is not merely adding another layer to the retail landscape but is reshaping our buying habits. The touch, feel, and see elements we deemed vital in purchasing decisions are undergoing a revolution as VR breaks physical limitations and broadens the spectrum of possibilities.

7.1. The New Paradigm: Shopping through VR

Imagine stepping into a furniture store, browsing through the different sections, testing out the comfort of the recliners, inspecting the quality of the wooden tables, and visualizing how they would fit into the layout of your house. Now imagine doing all this without stepping a foot outside your home. This is the reality that VR is bringing to the retail sector. By crafting immersive 3D shopping experiences, customers can now interact with products in ways unimaginable before. Brands can showcase their products in customizable virtual environments, allowing customers to make informed and personalized purchasing decisions. Customers can try on clothes, preview home furnishings in their space, or test drive cars, all digitally. This seamless and intuitive integration of technology is not merely an upgrade, but a reimagining of a fundamental human activity.

7.2. The VR Effect on Purchase Decisions

The power of VR lies not only in the revolutionary experience it provides but also in the profound effect it has on customer behavior and purchasing decisions. Shopping journeys powered by VR offer rich, immersive, and personalized experiences that significantly impact perceived product value and purchase intent. VR experiences can better satisfy the human need for exploration and novelty, thus strongly influencing customer satisfaction and loyalty. An approachable attempt at integrating VR into traditional customer service would be offering a 360-degree view of your products or a virtual tour of your physical store.

In comparison to other forms of online shopping, VR adds a level of interactivity and personalization that raises customer satisfaction and reduces purchasing risks. Customers can interact with products in ways similar to in-store shopping, minimizing the uncertainties associated with online shopping. Heightened customer satisfaction translates to increased consumer spending, forging a more positive relationship between a brand and its customers.

7.3. Cultivating Brand Image and Loyalty

VR allows brands to connect with their customers genuinely and creatively. Creating immersive brand experiences helps connect with customers on an emotional level, leading to stronger brand loyalty. Notably, Millenials and Generation Z, who value immersive experiences and proactive action, are more likely to be loyal to brands that provide such experiences.

In addition, VR can also significantly impact a brand's image. A brand adopting VR is perceived as cutting-edge, innovative, and customer-centric. This perceived modernity and innovation can significantly enhance a brand's reputation, attracting potential customers and retaining existing ones.

7.4. Looking Ahead: The Future of Shopping Behaviour

Considering these impacts, the adoption of VR in retail promises a transforming influence on consumer behaviour in the future. As technology becomes more advanced, accessible, and affordable, we can expect VR to become a dominant force in the retail industry.

Trips to physical stores might soon become a thing of the past as more consumers familiarize themselves with VR technology. Soon, our shopping might be done in sophisticated virtual malls, offering previously unimaginable levels of convenience and personalization. And as more companies recognize the potential of VR in retail, we can expect an investment surge in this technology in the years to come, both in terms of capital and innovation.

However, acknowledging the potent influence of VR isn't enough. Both consumers and retailers must understand its implications fully. We need to ensure that this new frontier isn't marked by the same pitfalls that plagued traditional retail environments. Being at the forefront of technological development, Virtual Reality has tremendous potential, but it is our responsibility to ensure that this potential is adequately and sustainably harnessed.

Virtual Reality is no longer a distant dream but a vibrant reality transforming shopping behaviours. The marriage of technology and retail offers a realm of exciting opportunities, and the phrase "seeing is believing" might soon be replaced with "experiencing is believing." And as we step into the new era of retail, the shopping illusions of yesterday are becoming the shopping reality of today.

The retail world is experiencing a digital disruption, and Virtual Reality stands at its helm. The integration of VR into shopping signifies more than technological innovation; it denotes an evolution of customer behaviour, a metamorphosis of retail landscapes, and a revolution of purchasing experiences. Welcome to the new era of retail, powered by Virtual Reality!

Chapter 8. Future Prospects: The Next Big Things in VR Shopping

As we march into the evolution of VR shopping, a multitude of potential lies embedded in this fascinating realm, promising immense growth and transformation. This technology has already made a notable impact on the retail sector, but it's just the beginning- a foretaste of the possible spectacle that can be achieved with widespread adoption, and strategic implementation.

8.1. Unshackled Shopping - Walking the Aisles Virtually

The advent of VR shopping will cascade into a platform for unlimited exploration. Shoppers won't just shop, they'll become adventurers. They can explore stores in virtual environments, pick up items, examine them from any angle, and even sample some products. One moment, they could be comparing tech gadgets in a New York City electronics store; the next, they could be touring a quaint Parisian boutique with only a few clicks.

By incorporating a detailed, realistic, and interactive 3D display of commodities, VR shopping is intended to provide an in-store shopping experience from the comfort of your home. The freedom to shop without geographical boundaries brings forth a new dawn in the field of shopping.

8.2. Tailored to Fit - Virtual Fitting Rooms

Imagine a world where you could try on any clothing item without actually having to change your outfit. With virtual reality, this will be the new norm. Virtual fitting rooms will allow customers to try on clothes, shoes, or accessories virtually with the help of 3D body models. It can also suggest the best fit, style, and color based on your appearance, preferences, and body type.

By enabling the customers to visualize how they'd look in different clothing styles and fits, virtual fitting rooms make for an effective shopping solution, eradicate chances of returning ill-fitted goods, and help make confident and worthwhile purchasing decisions.

8.3. An Augmented Reality - Revolutionizing Product Interactions

VR shopping won't just present a 360-degree view of products but will also allow the customer to interact with those products. With retail VR, consumers can potentially see how a sofa fits into their living room or test a potential recipe using virtual ingredients.

Through VR, the customers can gain first-hand experiences of utilizing the products in reality, bringing a new level of authenticity and transparency to the shopping experience. It creates another dimension of understanding that eliminates guesswork, bolsters consumer confidence, and invariably, boosts sales.

8.4. Personalized Shopping Assistants

Virtual shopping assistants are set to massively upgrade the customer service experience. These AI-powered entities can understand the customer's needs, preferences, and shopping patterns. They then make personalized recommendations based on their understanding. These assistants will be equipped to answer queries, provide additional product information, and even accompany customers during their entire shopping journey.

8.5. A More Inclusive Shopping Experience

VR technology can help retailers create a more inclusive shopping space by improving accessibility for those unable to physically visit stores. Via this platform, everyone has equal access to shopping spaces, opening up new opportunities for those with physical disabilities, the elderly, or those living in remote areas.

8.6. Streamlining the Supply Chain

Virtual reality won't just revolutionize consumers' shopping experiences, but will also streamline businesses' operations. By transforming processes like employee training and product design, it can drastically cut costs and increase efficiency.

8.7. Rethinking Advertisement and Marketing Strategies

VR offers an immersive environment where product interactions feel more real than traditional forms of advertisement. Advertisers and marketers can leverage this to create immersive marketing campaigns. Consumers can "use" the product virtually before deciding to purchase it, thus allowing brands to more effectively demonstrate the value of their offerings.

8.8. Conclusion

Whether we're ready or not, VR shopping is on the horizon and is set to redefine the retail landscape, from the consumers' shopping experience to retailers' business operations. It holds an ocean of possibilities, and the impacts stated above are just scratching the surface. For the tech industry, VR has moved from being an ambitious concept to a rich, dynamic platform that presents novel ways to augment customer experiences. We are, indeed, on the brink of a shopping revolution!

Chapter 9. Obstacles in VR Adoption and Their Potential Solutions

While virtual reality continues its march towards becoming mainstream, there are several hurdles in its path that may delay its widespread acceptance, particularly in the retail industry. However, with each problem comes a solution, and as technology evolves, many of these obstacles seem less daunting.

9.1. Technological Limitations

Currently, one of the prevailing issues hindering the wider adoption of virtual reality in retail is the technological limitations. While high-quality VR systems do exist, they're often expensive and require advanced computing capabilities far beyond what a standard user might possess. This results in an economic divide that restricts the broader adoption of VR technologies for an average customer.

Moreover, even with the high-end VR systems, issues like latency, motion sickness due to low frame rates or poorly developed content, and lack of sufficient resolution pose significant challenges. These technical hitches could lead to a less than satisfactory user experience, discouraging potential users.

Possible solutions involve continuous investment in research and development to enhance VR technologies. Major tech companies worldwide are engaging in a continuous quest to better this brand-new breed of experiential technology. As technology improves, the costs of production decrease, gradually making VR systems more accessible to the vast public. Furthermore, improved hardware specifications such as better display technology, higher frame rates, and low latency will contribute to overcoming motion sickness and latency.

9.2. User Experience and Usability

At the heart of VR lies the simple prerogative: creating a seamless, intuitive user experience. However, lack of familiarity with technology can pose a serious challenge. Certain users might find it difficult to navigate through the virtual environments, operate the VR controllers, or comprehend the VR interface.

Potential solutions include developing intuitive designs that cater to the varying degrees of tech-literacy levels of end-users. Businesses can employ user testing and feedback systems to iterate and improve their VR interfaces. Additionally, there should be efforts to provide user training to improve VR literacy, in-store user guidance, and readily available online tutorials.

9.3. Content Creation and Curation

Content is key in virtual reality experiences. The lack of attractive, compelling, and immersive content poses a significant obstacle in VR adoption in retail. Creating such content requires artistic skills, technical competence, and a deep understanding of the narrative techniques specific to VR.

However, the content creation landscape is quickly evolving, with various tools and platforms emerging that make creating VR content more approachable. Tech companies need to further simplify these tools, reach out to creators, and provide them with the necessary training and resources. Moreover, collaboration with digital agencies specializing in VR content creation can expedite the curation process of engaging content.

9.4. Health and Safety Concerns

While VR offers exciting opportunities, it is not without potential health risks. Extended use of VR headsets could lead to eyestrain, dizziness, or even temporary disorientation. Furthermore, moving around while wearing a VR headset might pose physical risks, such as bumping into objects or tripping over cables.

To address these issues, the development of reliable health and safety standards and regulations is crucial. These might include usage guidelines, such as recommended break times and use duration limits. It's also important to design VR systems with in-built safety measures that prevent users from moving beyond designated areas.

9.5. Societal Acceptance

Slow societal acceptance of VR technology is another obstacle. For many, VR is seen as a novelty or a gaming tool, rather than a platform for shopping or business.

To change this perception, businesses will need to educate the public about the potential of VR beyond gaming. This could be achieved through mass media campaigns, collaborative studies, and public demonstrations. Convenient, hands-on experiences via in-store VR kiosks could illustrate the practical uses of VR in a retail context.

In conclusion, while the journey towards widespread VR adoption is fraught with obstacles, it is not insurmountable. No doubt that the journey brings along several challenges, but it's worth remembering that the evolution of VR is a continuum, and with time and technological advancement, the barriers will eventually crumble. As solutions emerge to overcome these obstacles, the future of virtual reality in retail becomes not a question of 'if' but 'when'. The shopping revolution isn't simply on the horizon; it's already knocking on the door.

Chapter 10. Case Studies: Successful Applications of VR in Retail

From clothing stores to car dealerships, furniture showrooms to supermarkets, virtual reality is revolutionizing the retail industry. It provides businesses with a new avenue to engage consumers, enhance their shopping experience, and ultimately drive revenue. Let's dive into how a few noteworthy businesses have successfully incorporated VR into their retail strategies.

10.1. IKEA: Design Your Dream Home

IKEA, the famous Swedish home furnishings manufacturer, rolled out its VR showroom in 2016 giving customers the capability to visualize and experiment with different furniture arrangements without leaving their homes. Called the "IKEA VR Experience," customers use a VR headset like HTC Vive to virtually tour a well-equipped kitchen, change colours, rearrange appliances, and even alter their perspective to the viewpoint of a child or a tall person.

This application of VR has proved influential, not only enhancing customers' shopping experiences by allowing them to preview their IKEA-designed rooms but also promoting confidence in their purchase decisions.

10.2. Lowe's: Holoroom How To

American home improvement retailer Lowe's also leveraged VR to introduce 'Holoroom How To', a VR-based DIY training simulator.

This program was devised to educate customers about home improvement projects like tiling a shower. The initiative has proved successful, with statistics highlighting an almost 40% better recall compared to YouTube tutorial viewers.

By utilizing VR, Lowe's offers an immersive, hands-on learning experience for consumers providing greater consumer engagement and potentially increasing in-store sales as customers purchase DIY products confident in their ability to utilize them post-training.

10.3. Audi: VR Showrooms

Audi, the German luxury car manufacturer, turned to VR to transform their customers' car buying experience. The "Audi VR experience" allows customers to virtually customize their vehicle using a VR headset. Users can view potential vehicles in incredible detail, change car features, and take the car for a virtual test drive.

Audi's VR application has been successful in both boosting customer engagement and enabling dealerships to present a larger variety of vehicles, including both existing and concept models, without the need for extensive physical showrooms.

10.4. Alibaba: VR Shopping

Chinese retail giant Alibaba introduced 'Buy+' VR technology to elevate the consumer shopping experience. Using VR goggles, buyers can now browse for their favourite items in a virtual mall featuring brands like Target, Costco, and Gap. Through the Buy+ experience, shoppers can view items in 3D, interact with virtual salespersons, and even watch a fashion show before deciding on their purchase.

The addition of the Buy+ VR experience significantly enhanced customer engagement for Alibaba by providing shoppers with a more interactive and immersive retail environment.

These are just a few of the many instances where VR technology has been employed successfully in the retail sector. Each example demonstrates different techniques on how VR was customized to meet specific retail sector needs, and there's no doubt that the possibilities for future application are limitless.

Whether it's altering the way we buy furniture, helping us improve our DIY skills, revolutionizing the car purchasing process, or turning online shopping into an immersive, interactive experience, VR is drastically changing the face of retail. As more retailers adopt this technology, we can anticipate even more innovative applications that will continue to redefine the shopping experience.

Chapter 11. Endless Aisles: The Virtual Shopping Experience of Tomorrow

In the business of retail, aisles have forever played a pivotal role. Reminiscent of a theater stage, they serve as the canvas where products come alive, generate curiosity, and eventually drive purchases. Virtual Reality (VR), owing to its capacity for sculpting unrestricted, moldable environments, is setting the stage for an evolution in this paradigm. The advent of 'Endless Aisles' echoes a monumental shift, propelling consumers into the future of immersive, uncompromising, and highly personalized shopping experiences.

11.1. Immersive Worlds Crafted around the Consumer

VR transcends the spatial limitations of physical retail stores, allowing businesses to position unlimited inventory within 'Endless Aisles'. This unveils a new spectrum of opportunities to present products in a way that's molded around the individual preferences, buying history, and behavioral patterns of consumers. Through precise data analytics, businesses can personalize each customer's VR journey.

Imagine standing on a high-street adorned with designer brands, a dense forest with outdoor gear, or even a galaxy far away with the latest sci-fi merchandise - all from the comfort of your home. Exemplifying the ethos of customer-centricity, businesses can construct wide-ranging environments that resonate personally with their target audiences, creating a profound bond that extends beyond the immersive virtual shopping experience.

11.2. Revolutionary Product Interaction

Delving into the 'Endless Aisles' of VR shopping goes beyond static viewing. It introduces a dynamic, interactive model of discovery. Customers can effortlessly reach out, grab, study, and even try products, appreciating their details from every angle without the physical constraints traditionally experienced.

Think of trying out camping gear in the midst of a virtual rainforest, the powerful roar of wildlife encircling you. Or perhaps sampling a lipstick shade in an extravagant dressing room of a Parisian chateau, experiencing the product as an extension of a desired lifestyle. This elaborate sense of believability is a prominent sales accelerator, contributing to increased customer satisfaction and reduced return rates, directly impacting the bottom line.

11.3. 'Smart' Personalized Recommendations

Another transformative prospect of VR 'Endless Aisles' brings to the table is the concept of 'smart' personalized recommendations. As shoppers navigate the virtual store, the advanced AI algorithms track their interactions, capturing attention spans, product preferences, and reactions to different stimuli.

This digital profiling facilitates delivery of bespoke product recommendations, emulating the intelligence of a skilled salesperson. A customer studying camping stoves might be advised a lantern or a utility knife - enhancing the potential for cross-selling and up-selling. More than a mere sales tool, these 'smart' recommendations also add value to the customer's shopping journey, making the interaction more efficient, enjoyable, and enriching.

11.4. Enriching Social Interactions

VR provides an avenue to recreate social dynamics within 'Endless Aisles', replacing the often isolating experience of online shopping. Users can shop together, try out clothes in mutual virtual dressing rooms, exchange opinions and even capture selfies, reiterating the social aspect of traditional shopping.

These experiences provide tangible emotional touchpoints for consumers, helping foster brand loyalty. The VR shopping model thus transcends beyond an experiential novelty to a tangible strategy for building a vigorous customer-brand relationship.

11.5. Overcoming the Barriers

Despite the captivating prospects, the concept of VR shopping and its 'Endless Aisles' does face certain challenges. Foremost among these are hardware requirements, the necessity for robust internet connectivity, and the ever-prominent issue of cyber-security.

It's crucial for businesses to collaborate with tech companies, fostering innovations in compressing VR data, refining security protocols, and making VR hardware more accessible. Only with diligent efforts and strategic partnerships can the full potential of VR in retail be truly unleashed.

The revolution of 'Endless Aisles' isn't a vague possibility of the future but an active transformation impacting the retail industry today. By bringing forth a highly personalized, visually impressive, and socially engaging shopping journey, it offers consumers an unmatched retail experience, while providing businesses a brand new stage to impress upon and connect with their customers. As Virtual Reality evolves, the future of 'Endless Aisles' is likely to become even more integrated, natural, and customary in our daily lives.